O Damn!

Poems of Age

O Damn!

Poems of Age

Robb Thomson

Many thanks to my daughter, Judy Thomson, for her insightful line by line editing of the manuscript.

Contents

I

Prologue

There are many paths
in old age,

but in every one
looms the question

what is it all about?

HIDDEN

The iridescent wing conceals the hunter bird,
a shallow wave veils the deep,
just as a smile masks a soul in pain,
and dread lies under a dusting of love.

THE WILL OF THE POEM

A poet is an optimist
Who,
      clutching a wisp of thought,
      or something seen
      in an odd light,
Thinks a poem
      can be made of it
      by following a subconscious
      guide as it makes
Its devious way
      along the connections of mind,

Till the poem wanders
      into a place,
Where a self,
      long sought,
      lives secluded
      in a cave of the spirit
Unlit before.

To Live

Is to learn to fail
without surrender,

so the next round
is undetermined.

Robb Thomson

To Love

Is to float in the silent
river of being,

content it will find
the ocean on its own.

5

Two Visions

Broad bands
    some vertical
    and one flat horizon-maker
All colored in desert tones
    of tans, purples, and oranges
    fade into one another
    to mock precise truth.
With the desert's patience, this painting
    leads me gently into and out
    of myself as I follow its shifting hues —

Until, still in hazy reverie,
My eye drifts alongside to a
    fishing boat as it emerges
    from the mists of early dawn
    and slowly turns in the tide
    on a woodblock print.
My spirit idles on its deck
    as I unfold from trance
    to prepare for the day to be.

Dreams of the Young

She slowly wakens,
and weaves her dreams into designs
of her own will, but then tears
out the unfinished cloth, and begins anew,
hoping the fit and color will be better.

New designs flash
faster than fingers can follow.
For the void from which they emerge
is vast and the choice endless.
But there is only one life to be made,
so she sits testing what it is like to be this or that,
and wonders why
one choice is better than another.

Undeterred by the mess
her elders have made,
she will thrive on risk
of her own,

marveling the while at people who live
in perfect grace,
whose tragedies line their faces
but not their souls.

THE SEARCH

In a din of frantic dissonance,
we demand our separate rights.

Yet strain to find a harmony
to relieve the estrangement
bramded in our faces.

FRIEND

From the stillness
of my hushed psyche,
a presence nods
when I ask if I am really real.

He links me to the world
of feel and affection,
and we often chuckle over
the joke of being alive.

But when devils
possess and goad him,
I am tangled in his terror,
as we spin through blackness
seizing one another in frantic embrace.

When the storms quieten,
I gently wipe his trembling brow,
and the joke becomes our joy.

RIVER RENEWED

As the reservoir is emptied for repairs
the river gurgles with joy
and its dry bed returns to life,
while rare rains wash
its parched banks.

The happy sounds bring out people
with their dogs, and the river path,
like the river itself,
sounds with an unaccustomed lightness.
The trees also dress for the party,
and their fall greens and yellows add
their color to the fête.

People relax in their ancient place
in Nature's arms,
and under a faultless sky,
the world laughs.

DUENDE

Unrest clasps my soul,
as the perfect predator,
known only by premonition,
strides round me in the dark
to cage me in a finite world.

Until I blur his vision with
the explosive fire of dance,
and my spirit vaults into the beyond
to cast back slivers
of that further world

whispering of home.

TREES IN FALL

The trees along our river
nap after a Summer's labor,
and their yellowness drips
in relief to the ground,
where it renews a welcoming earth.

Water, this Eden's ambrosia,
flows off the mountain
making the only sound
to celebrate the touch
of the world-spirit come to earth.

Standing in separation,
I pray permission
to join this paradise
and share the joy
of its completeness,

Horseshoe

The future is a sneaky bastard
with death hidden
in his boxer's glove like a horseshoe,
ready to deal me a knockout blow —

when he can catch me.

AMEN

A dying sun
lays a soft hand
on a slowing heart
consoled by an unthought prayer
as it
sighs through parted lips.

II

Portrait of a Spring

Through earth's lips
I giggle my way into the light,
after feeling my way through rock crevices
in the dark.

Now released, I roll and tumble
into the vale where feeding
fish wait to wash their thirsty gills
and long legged-buggy things test my surface tension.

In the sun, and no longer alone,
I stretch and frolic
with others trickling down
the mountainside.

Until, flowing into the flat, my pace slows,
as again and again, loathsome slop
splashes my face from the leering
mouths of gushing gargoyles along the banks.

Now burdened and violated,
I empty into a welcoming sea,
Where the sun promises a cleansing ride
Back to the top again

For another breathless slide.

THE ENLIGHTENMENT

Gallileo said "Watch the ball roll!"
Newton did — and set it to math.
The secrets of the world
opened like a flower,
and the power of the whole earth
bowed to mankind.

Released from Nature's bounds,
and ecstatic with new riches,
the people scattered cities everywhere,
and cavorted over land and sea
till the earth groaned and the animals hid.
Discarded junk concealed earth's beauties,
and the people's love turned to drink.

Their shriveled souls tried
to transplant a little enlightenment
from the outer world
to the equally vast inner one,

But have not yet found out how.

NURTURING ALEXANDERS

Many boys dream of being
Alexander when they grow up,
and thrill to the knowledge
that enemies in their thousands will die
in the defeats in store for them.

Some even become his heirs,
learning how to bind others
to their charisma
with the thrill
of blood to be poured in their name.

In the end, as he counts all those bodies
in their stacked mounds,
what has any Alexander
made of his own humanity?

And can the world, now peopled
from edge to edge,
abide the hatred engendered
in the hearts of the living
by his millions murdered?

And what about those boys?

2050

He tinkers with the program
and tries again, but is still not sure
his computer is conscious.
This machine can do almost everything
any human can do,
and it says it loves him.

But how can he be certain
the damned thing is telling the truth?

ANGRY SEA

A thousand miles
of pent up sea breaks
on the defiant rocks
in a quarrel that goes back
to the beginning of time.

There is no winner apparent to me.
I remember what the sea
has done to those rocks
over the millenia,
and that the rocks call
on vast underground reserves
from the earth's mantle
to push the sea back towards Asia
inches at a time —
its patience sometimes broken
when the earth's crust ruptures
and the sea retreats in sudden surprise.

This must be the animosity
left over from the battle between
the Olympians and the Titans
when the world began,

and humans are still beside the point.

THE BUTTERFLY EFFECT

It is said the world,
especially its human side,
is so nonlinear and quirky,
that small acts can
have large consequences.

But how is a temper outburst
or protest by a few determined people
timed to just the moment
all humanity is perched on a knife edge?

ZOMBIES AT THE DOOR

A cyborg zombie stands at our door,
to take from our hands the work
they used to do making things
traded for food,
things that gave those hands delight
in thingly feels
and whose worked forms
gave beauty to our eyes.

How does one now search out the joy
found in making gifts
that touch the soul of humanity?
Are there new kinds of gifts
no one knows yet how to make?
And if so, how is one
to learn the new crafts required?

Perhaps this view is too prosaic —
If these zombies are the forerunner
of a future race humanity
will learn to fashion
to populate the universe with consciousness,

just tell us,
so, as their tutors, we can endure
the indignity and frustration
of giving them first lessons
in the joy of love.

THE GREAT GAME

In an earlier age,
he would have been
a tyrant, with lesser beings
bowing to feed his bloated vanity;
every lust satisfied
at the turn of a finger.

But now things are subtler,
and he knows that although
sheer delight can be had
by cheating the unwary, eventually
the bastards catch on and gang up on you.

Greater power comes
when he cloaks himself
as the people's man,
while giving small sops
to the idiots close enough to know.

So the trick is knowing when
to cash in
before the secret is out —
You can hear the suckers
scream as you close the door.

But as he grows older,
he sees the masters

conceal the hook very deep,
profit for a lifetime,
and end their days
sainted in the press.

And he can't determine
if they are true members
of the guild to the end,
or have ratted along the way —

They drop no clues.

KIDS!

They dribble through the door.
Some have been here before,
and others are uncertain
about what is to be found here.
All hope there will be
help with incorrigible
math or science topics
which they cannot get from a parent
who works two jobs and is maybe
clueless about the subject too.

Some are sure these classes
are just punishment of kids
by elders, and they build a grudge.
A small group are not so sure
and suspend suspicion —
until excitement builds
as they get it.

I am a foreigner here.
These kids' brains
move faster than mine,
and their culture is
different from the one I grew up in.
So, like any visitor in a strange place,
I am intensely aware of my
otherness.

What brings me here is
knowing that growing up
is a huge challenge only the young
have the strength and courage for,
and if they shirk or fail,
a whole generation will suffer.

But more
is the awareness that these kids,
though far from my own family circle,
are buds on the same human organism
that nourished my own flowering
with a love so critical
to my own becoming.

TWO PATHS

He is ecstatic as he learns
to simulate the stock market
and the weather.
The ease with which he can explore
alternate versions of those worlds
makes him a god, and he delights
in his view from Olympus.

He can hardly wait to get the PhD
that will entitle him to manipulate
real accounts and real projects,
and is aware of the open arms
that await the end of his novice days.

She writes fiction and is enrolled
in the history of civilization.
There are few numbers here,
but before her eyes,
the evolution of a shared humanity
from forces welling up from its collective will
hints at a beauty that stuns her.

For her, no open arms beckon
from the high keeps of power or finance,
for she can only offer the beauties she finds
on the inlets and shallows of her own being.

But she knows the foods she harvests there
are essential nutrients for the human soul,
and she easily makes the choice that
determines her future.

The tools he fashions are at bottom no different
from those laboriously napped
from stone into an edge those eons ago,
and the consequences of his industry
will be no less momentous than theirs.

She makes no tools but often uses them —
her interest is the inner being
of humanity, and what it is trying to become.

To War No More

You and I are gods in diapers
with a psyche hammered
to a bent shape over
a blacksmith's anvil
by a will to dominate
inherited from our recent
origins in a raw earth.

But dominance over all things,
human and other,
has driven us
to a biblical end of days —
to be eluded only
by a will
desperate to live,
and thus to love,
propagating its own future
from scratch.

III

DEPRESSION FAMILY

In reverie, I stand
    across the street
    from the tiny house
    where I grew up
    in depression times.
Memory pierces its walls
    to the living ghosts inside,
And I try to feel the desperation eating
    the insides of those parents of mine
    facing unemployment at any moment.
How did they do it,
    with children sleeping on the back porch?

What I don't remember at all is feeling
    that desperation.
Learning instead ways of dealing with little —
    selling tomatoes to go to the circus
    selling magazines to get a bike
    selling newspapers to go to college.
Building little things into bigger things
    and never giving up.

Thank you, my dears
    for not showing us
    that crushing desperation
    but just enough of its distant threat
To color lives of hope for us,
    and give us the habits
    to make them possible.

Kitchen Tables

The first
was a giant roof with legs
I could run under to get away
from the big world.
I whirled around
one leg and launched myself
to another in the corner,
from where I could view
kitchen-land with all the detachment
any small boy needed.

It was a favorite hiding place
for hide and seek,
because back in that corner,
I was invisible
from the front room
where the game always started,
and I could race IT back
to base when he turned
to look in the pantry
on the other side of the kitchen.

But out of my control,
the table grew inexorably smaller,
and began to shake dangerously
if I whirled around a leg.

Evicted from beneath,
I began to look over its edge
at the things on its top,
among which was
that most delicious food of all —
the lickings left in the mixing bowl
after the cake batter
had gone into the baking pans.

There were smaller tables
I would later haul into other kitchens —
finally a round one,
handed down from the dining room
dominated our kitchen,
and its swelling collection
of nicks and scars, like the growth marks
of a child on a door jamb, became the visible
symbol of a family in motion.

THE NEW BUICK

When the Appletons got their new '33 Buick,
my family was invited for a ride.
I sat deep in the middle of the front seat,
with my view out the windshield limited
to the naked, silver-plated Venus
who stuck up in mid-air above the radiator.

A 'straight eight,' the engine seemed
as long as a football field, where, mounted
astride those eight thrusting pistons,
the goddess sailed in front of us.

With the dashboard dials dancing in my lap,
the alluring lady in front threw control to me,
and I joined my male brethren in a covenant
with the world force —
making us rulers of the earth,
if we could but tame the primal potency
hurtling from under that hood.

The Kill

I was ten years old
when Dad asked me to help him
butcher the kid goat for our meat locker.
It was hung by its hind legs
from the roof of the goat pen,
eyes wide with fear and bleating wildly,
when Dad hit him hard
where his spine entered his head,
and the kid went silent and rigid.
Dad then slit his throat in a quick
swipe, and as blood ran into the
waiting bucket, I fell to the ground
in a dead faint.

A constant ache in my soul
began on that morning,
when, falling, I realized the gentle world
I had known, whose permeating love
had been the central breath of my life,
had a dual face, constantly turning
this way and that —

and that it was not yet truly human.

Leaving Home

I was seventeen,
and as the desert scrub and telephone poles
rushed past me on the train out of town,
I looked beyond them to the mountains
sheltering our town,
and remembered the days spent
exploring their secrets.

This landscape was like a revered grandfather,
and generated in me a loyalty
that would remain forever
stamped on my being.

Wherever this train could take me
those feelings would be in my deepest pocket
where I would roll them in my fingers,
like the smooth stones I used to collect.

But even through all this finality and loss,
my spirit was firmly attached
to the locomotive's headlamp,
and from a place, unknown before,

I laughed.

DAYDREAMS

When I was a kid
I drew pictures of the huge
air ship I would design
using the principle demonstrated
by my blown up balloon
as it flitted around the room deflating.

I dreamed of the fleets of those ships
I would command,
and how I would defeat
all who dared confront me.

At other times, I would dream
of the great discoveries I would make,
and the insights I would reveal
to an astonished world
like dispensations from a great king.

The universe had a clarity then,
as if, on command, some huge genie
had told me its inner secrets.

Those dreams still color my days
with out-of-focus purpose,
and a shrunken genie still whispers
that we and mystery are one.

Tea Party in the Attic

"We love our nigras,"
my white haired uncle exclaimed
from his seat across the restaurant table,
and he said they loved him, too.
He went on to upbraid me for deserting
my Southern-leaning home
for brain washing in the hated North
at a loathsome liberal university.

This was the Old South still talking in 1942,
and, suddenly face to face with it,
I was deeply shocked by its evil banality.

Even though my mother had insisted
on this visit to her Mississippi roots
and the brother Judge she adored,
we fought with the give-no-quarter tenacity
of the two generations we represented.

And we both knew he had lost,
for he was the one with
uncertain gait and failing authority.

I wonder now if,
under the damning judgment
his side was to suffer,
he went into the prison of History,
with remorse — did truth ever dawn?

I suspect no,
that his beloved nigras
still shone brightly to him,
and that he went into that cell
to spawn new visions of wornout ways
from his ghostly seat in our ancestral latency.

GROWING UP

When I was a kid, true Americans
had white skins, and we knew
the future belonged just to us.
Our superiority was not due
exactly to our race, but to
something subtler having to do
with our industry and hard work,
and may have had something
to do with the Protestant religion.

Though we were very proud of
Joe Louis when he defeated Max Schmelling,
and Jesse Owens when he won
the Olympics and tweaked Hitler's nose,
we were puzzled about Blacks,
and much more comfortable
with those of lighter skins
and thinner lips.

In university, I became an easy
convert to Liberalism, and the idea
that intellectual capacity was evenly
distributed between the races,
though I didn't act that way
up close and personal very easily.
The final steps came only
when a black man became my son in law,

his daughter my granddaughter.

Untouched by that distant garbage,
I loved her as my own,
and her instinctive welcome into her own
new life was a gift
precious beyond telling.

SQUIRRELS

We had squirrels in our attic
who entered from the roof
after jumping the open space
from our backyard tree.

When I cut away the limbs
on the house side,
I watched from the back door
to see the result.

The big squirrel made a gigantic
leap to the roof and,
with chest pumped out,
turned to the youngster left behind.

A loud and extended chatter
then took place, with Mama
gesticulating and jumping up and down
from the roof,

while youngster answered
in kind from the tree in a higher key.
He would crouch for the jump,
but, unable to release the twig,

would merely twitch his tail in fear.
Alas, he was stuck on the limb

and no scolding parent
could dislodge him.

Finally, Mama emitted a disgusted
shriek at her cowardly
and disobedient offspring
and jumped back to the tree.

Where, without another look
at her child, she ran
to the other end of the yard
and abandoned the roof for good.

EMILY

Our backpacks from the previous day's hike
were still scattered on the floor of the lean-to
when a young deer browsed noisily in the early
dawn among the trees just beyond
our tamped campfire.

She peered, with an innocence unsullied
by man's predation at the still waking visitors
to her woods —
while, whispering in warm
sleeping bags, our children excitedly dubbed her
Emily,
and invited her to a breakfast romp.

After a too-close encounter,
she would scamper off, showing
her magnificent white flag, and then return,
teasingly, as she shyly peeked through the trees
taking us always on her own terms.

She became the sprite of our forest,
and returned us to childhood metaphors,
when Pogo and his friends taught us
the deep ways of a truly human world
run by animals speaking English.

Miraculous Dot

The angst of being alone
in their skins, with the anxieties
also harbored there, stares back at me
from behind the street masks
of the people I meet on my morning walk.

I search among them for signs of the Fabled One,
and now and then find the imprint
of the divine touch shining
like a Hindu bindi on an unmasked brow.

Discovered, their smile
lights up my world,
and enables me to dispense
unasked love with abandon,

till,
my limited capacities exhausted,
I revert to weaving through the crowd
looking for that reddish dot.

A GENTLE HAND

A girlish face once greeted me
with parted lips
waiting for the subtle touch
only she could
engender.

As years passed,
the beguiling myths of her youth
stole away,
and the blackness
of that treachery filled her face.

Innocence turned to fire in her eyes
as she realized
what would be required of her will
to soothe and make malleable
an unexpectedly harsh world.

But her will was betrayed
by the limits of a human psyche,
and in the end, not yet strangled
by Alzheimers, her eyes softened
as she kissed a gently offered hand
in the falling shadow.

To Junius

When we peddled tomatoes from our wagon
to the neighbors for tickets to the circus,
    we didn't think of this.
When you brought home the first S. E. Posts,
and we went from house to house
with Dad watching in the car —
"You wouldn't like to buy a
Saturday Evening Post, would you?"
    We didn't think of this.
When we cleared the vacant lot
for you to play ball,
    this day was still far in the future.

From your hospital bed
you look at us
with the grin I first saw
when you sold that long ago tomato
and again,
when the clown tipped his hat to you.

It is an aged grin now,
flowing un–dammed over valleys of wrinkles
from a deep spring of joy,
infectious to all who see in it
a reflection of love,
dispensed with effortless grace.

In reply, we bless with a flower's caress
from our circle of endearment,
and go with you
into the sunset as far
as tethered bodies allow.

STARTING OVER

Elizabeth Spencer, a writer of short stories,
has a new book, *Starting Over*.
People smile at her 92 years,
but I think she is serious —
onto something important,
with not a minute to spare.

I know the feeling.

I too have lived much linear time,
but days stretch as far as the stars,
and each one is dense
with the possibility
of precious new meaning
to paste on an edifice never completed.

Robb Thomson

Dead of Night

At night
as my mind folds inward to sleep,
my conscious self
is prone to set watch
on the light switch
in fear that if allowed to trip
my wayward mind might lose its way
in the ghettos of sleep.

His Mentor

Like all boys,
he felt no hint of the great Teacher
who would one day shape his life beyond
anything a boy could conceive.

He dreamed only
of leading a space fleet,
of flying by willing it,
of being President,
and nothing intrigued him like
the seductive dance of nature,
whose veils concealed vast worlds
just waiting for him.

The first hints came
when a pig-tailed girl in sixth grade
always beat him at arithmetic,
when he couldn't break out of the pack
in high school,
when he busted his gut in university math
and still missed an A.
But through all that, down deep,
he knew he was exceptional.

Till he found himself in a crowd of guys
just back from Los Alamos
on their way to Nobel Prizes and other fame,

in a university department
headed by the greatest of the great professors.
It was all or nothing,
and for him
nothing.

He stood
shriveled and naked
before his nemesis,
the greatest of all Teachers —
failure,

a teacher without syllabus,
a merciless mentor.
All those early warnings now haunted him,
all his senses tasted bitter from
the lies that had guided him,
and he was a shunned alien
in the only world he knew.
He yearned to get as far away as he could,
and Alaska beckoned.

But still at the center of his psyche
was a rooted kernel
yearning for the skill to take blows
without giving up,
who longed to build a life of beauty

fashioned from moment to moment
from the odds and ends presented.

What he didn't see at the time
was the stream of ghouls and goblins
being deflected back to his flaming hell
by the love of the gentle girl now at his side;
and in the hooded smile of his Teacher,
he glimpsed the strength
he most needed would come from the grace
she could grant him.

The great shock he had sustained
never completely receded
and occasionally appeared
as a bottomless chasm
when he least expected it.
But his psyche was no longer
the helpless naif it had been —
he had learned to scale
slippery chasm sides.

And the sere Teacher
had become his most precious mentor.

IV

O Damn!

Here I am
reduced to the strength of a small child
with a pill regimen that would choke a goat,
when I get the message
the other guests are going
and it is time to leave.

Hell,
the fun has just begun.

BEAUTY

Across the vastness between species
the flower,
wrapped in its blue,
instructs me in the intimate
secrets of beauty;

a wisdom so deep and direct
that when I whisper of love,
my sighs
are the sighing of a flower.

Robb Thomson

STAR BRIGHT

Lovely star I see tonight,
in all that lonely wonder
has anyone else
seen thy tiny light?

A Hint of Laughter

Aged, silent and gnarly,
a tree stands in my memory,
its shape distinctive with regrowth
spanning scars
from the storms of its years.

Its inherited strength
is there to see,
but this tree is tougher, broader and taller
than its brothers,
and stands when many have gone.

In my awe before it,
something
lurking in its soul
laughs with me.

A Question

Do I fancy a universe determined by its beginning
or one governed by chance?
How about one governed by a God I can't grasp?

Or would I wish a universe that
leans toward purpose felt
but never fully known?

INVENTING A WORLD

Protected from the crushing pressure
of an utterly foreign world,
my spirit looks out from its bathysphere
at teeming life.

And I imitate that world
with an internal puppet show
animated with stories built on
the human invention of love,
and a wistful hope that it
actually has a counterpart out there.

The Beginning in the End

What we call the beginning is often the end
and to make an end is to make a beginning.

T. S. Eliot "Little Gidding"

In my beginning,
the gentle stars
— angels of the universe —
bent down from their remoteness

to convert their mystery
into brotherhood.

They took my small love
and magnified it,
suffusing
my entire world.

All things were open
to my innocence,
and my curiosity
found no locked doors.

But as I deepened my search
new challenges
like arithmetic
proved more securely packaged,

and the true secrets of how
the world is put together
were wrapped in subtlety
far from a boy's ken.

Even the people around me
developed mixed-up reasons
for what they did,
and later I had no answers
to my children's questions.

In this way did the cold
brighter stars further out
remain remotely foreign,
and imprison me in finiteness.

Within such confines,
what meaning could be found
that was not also small and incomplete?
And doubt moved into my psyche to stay.

In the end, a chastened and bruised self
turned back to its origins
in the warm fellowship of those near stars,
and I determined
only to wander from them in small steps —

to create new constellations
from their heavenly patterns,
and open new fields of human tenderness
from their loving embrace.

THE BRUTES

There is howling and screaming
as my genes fight for my attention
from the lidded pit
where I keep my biology.

The eldest ones, locked deeply
in my roots, know only
constant warfare with everyone in sight,
while the younger enjoin
my love of neighbor and homeland.

I keep the misshapen oldsters
closely chained
but am also wary
of the two-faced juniors —

for there was a day when
I thrilled at the fading
eyes of my tribe's enemy
as my fist closed round his throat,
and his slowly fell from mine,
all to unanimous cheering from the pit.

I am left in a helpless sweat
when, in dream, I relive that day,
and my beasts deny me
another ending.

So I sit
patiently spinning the gossamer bonds
of a softer humanity
with which to entangle my brutes
in a soothing cocoon of communion
to ease their anguish.

FREE WILL

Since anyone could think,
　　people have wondered if
　　their actions were their own
　　or someone else's.

First was a God who could have ruled
　　but didn't.
Then predestination was invented
　　and we were off on the other track.

Finally differential equations
　　predicted the path of the universe,
　　and the whole of the future
　　was contained in its beginning.

Is, then, the free
living force that gives me meaning
but an illusion?

STAGES OF OLD AGE

Becoming old is a process
starting somewhere around 40
when the kids are teenagers,
and a generational perspective
hardens.

It continues with retirement
when, if lucky, a pension
graces our living needs,
and we can volunteer
or just spend our days at golf.

But on golf course
or looking into the eyes of grandkids,
we face suddenly
the question of what it is all about.

So in the dotage of my old age,
I turn to poetry
to scan for hints of a largeness
I can only feel, but not fathom,

that cradles me in my smallness,
and laughs with me
at such a puny understanding
as mine.

Two Birds

who live
in the leafless chest-high bush
in front of my door
flit nervously among its twigs
to get as much protection
as they can from
late winter cold and snow.

They seldom fly when
I pass, but nervously chatter
and squint, ready to jump
if necessary, while guarding
an ancient nest, visible
only when you look closely
at a shadow deep in the bush
for intentional form.

Though wingèd
and, capable of spanning continents
they choose to make
a world in my bush
and the garden patio in front of my apartment,
where everything required
for a bird-happy life
lies only a few wing flaps away.

Can I learn from them
as my world constricts
from the size of the planet
to a few steps beyond this same courtyard?
Unlike my bird friends,
I require an entire civilization
to nourish and give me meaning,
and I fear my humanity will be diminished
by the measure of this patio.

But, with a wink at them,
I think "Only if I let it."

FINALITY

Evolution is purposeless, they say,
but consciousness,
as its finest accomplishment,
is haunted by meaning,
even if it doesn't know what it is.

If that is not Purpose,
it certainly
is a giant search for one.

TOUCH

In reverie,
I revisit a presence
who sits, silent and Buddha-like,
at the center of my awareness
absorbing me
into a sense of being.

When my focus wanders beyond,
your vision appears
with an electric jolt
as our touch opens each to the other —
brother or sister discovered,
linked through the living sky.

GHOSTS

Rising to the morning ritual
of my breakfast,
dense clouds of ghosts
crowd around
to monitor my menu
and exact thanks
for finding what nourishes,
and the means to provide it.

They circle my head like a halo
at each station of the day,
and when I can remember,
I raise my eyes briefly
in acknowledgement,

for, unlike all other life,
it is not to biology
my debt is owed,
but to the love
tendered by generations
of my own kind —

Robb Thomson

a collective love lighting the darkness
of our essential smallness
and groping failure,
bent on fulfilling a human destiny
only felt and never fully known.

Fluctuation

Of all the sperm seeking the egg,
only one made it,
and of all the people who could be,
I am he.
Like the flicker of an ember
rising from a camp fire,
I glow for a moment and disappear,
and yet in that moment
a whole world is made to be.

The improbable mystery of you,
and the other worlds of you
is beyond understanding.
But your touch and the love it passes
feeds the fire that
instead of blood
is pumped to every atom of my soul,

and I live in you and you in me —
lovers
who found each other at the beginning
of possibility
and together form the élan
that impels the universe to be.

Robb Thomson

Nature Unmasked

Into a frightful day
the new volcano belched
its undigested vomitus
and fumes
from unexplored strata of hell.

The sun disappeared
from this side of the earth
in clouds of ash, as lava
flamed across the land
like a giant oil well out of control,
transferring inner mantle
into new crustal geology.

All is peaceful now, with life
long since reasserted in the tuff,
but the old drama of earth
gone berserk stares at us
from an upended horizon,

and on an underwater map,
we can peer at a vast crater formed
even earlier,
when the whole earth shuddered.

Thus does our mother subtly
veil her powers.

INCANDESCENCE

Poorly sheltered in a body
    dehydrated by the desert of life,
I hold, quivering in cupped hands,
    the pure incandescence
    of fragile naked self.

I am linked thus to the larger world of being —

flesh
enlivening
bones of a starred universe.

EPILOGUE

I saw two coffins on a mound —
one so dense,
it sank
like a stone in water.

But attend
the pale aura of the second,
Oh Grave, for it
is mystery.

About the Author

Robb Thomson grew up in El Paso, Texas during the mid 20's to early 40's of the last century. He was educated at the University of Chicago and at Syracuse University, where he received a PhD in Physics. He spent a career in research and teaching on the faculties of the University of Illinois (Urbana) and The State University of New York (Stony Brook) and at the National Institute of Standards and Technology.

Thomson lives in Santa Fe, NM, and writes poetry because, as the most powerful language we have, it is a joyful guide to one's unfamiliar self, and an equally enlightening guide to the outside world we only thought we knew.

He has written two earlier books of poems, *Arranging the Constellations*, published by Mercury Heartlink, and *Centering the Pieces*, published by Robb Thomson.

CPSIA information can be obtained at www.ICGtesting.com
Printed in the USA
LVOW11s0113131014

408421LV00002B/3/P